WEB
-TO-
PRINT

A STEP-BY-STEP GUIDE FOR IMPLEMENTING WEB-TO-PRINT TECHNOLOGY

ABHISHEK AGARWAL
NIDHI AGRAWAL

MC2Books, a division of McGrewGroup, Inc.
1055 Richfield St. Aurora, CO 80011 USA

ISBN: 978-1-893347-09-0

MC2 Books is a member of McGrewGroup, Inc.

MC2 Books are available at special discounts for bulk purchases.

Please contact McGrewGroup, Inc. at 1055 Richfield St. Aurora, Colorado, 80011 or find us on the web at

http://www.mcgrewgroup.com/

Acknowledgments

With more than 20 years of combined experience in the printing industry, we realized we should write a step-by-step guide for our customers and printers from all verticals to understand and successfully implement a web-to-system. We had one aim - to help everyone fully understand what web-to-print means for their business and how they can implement it successfully.

It took us three months of numerous discussions, copywriting, and editing to finally develop this book of knowledge.

We would like to acknowledge the following people for encouraging us and assisting us in the creation of this book:

Our clients for believing in our solutions and sharing their success stories with the world. Our brilliant team for their dedication to building world-class software solutions and helping us understand various phases of implementation and suggestions to describe each one in details in the book.

Our daughter Aananya for enthusiasm and being a source of constant motivation for us to finish this book.

Pat McGrew for her encouraging feedback on the book, sharing her vision and her insightful editorial skills in bringing this new edition.

Rita Estevinha Silva for the new book cover design.

Lastly, we dedicate this book to our parents for their unconditional love and support and for making us believe that nothing is IMPOSSIBLE!

CONTENTS

Preface

The internet supports the growth of e-commerce as a retail platform for many goods and services across the globe. In 2021, all online sales accounted for 19.6 percent of retail sales worldwide. Statista predicts this will grow to a quarter of all sales by 2025. (Statista)

The rise in sales is inevitable. In 2020, Statista says that more than two billion people shopped online, which isn't surprising since consumers can shop 24/7, access more commodities and suppliers, and choose from the cheapest deals. They use mobile channels and voice-activated smart speakers to make purchases while enjoying the convenience of avoiding brick-and-mortar shops. And they can get it fast. The rise of e-commerce also accelerated the demand for next-day and same-day delivery services.

Part of that growth is in printed products of all types. Most of those products result from an interaction with web-to-print (W2P) technology.

Today, a simple search allows consumers to browse through hundreds of web-to-print websites - each of them offering great service and value. Not just that, they can choose from both custom print and print-ready items from unbranded suppliers at the lowest price.

The user experience enabled by web-to-print technology can't be ignored. It builds an environment of convenience for all consumers. But before we delve into that, let us get down to the basics. The following chapters walk you through the processes associated with web-to-print technology. There are exercises included to help you build your path to success.

UNDERSTANDING
WEB-TO-PRINT

What is Web-To-Print?

Web-to-print technology lets companies offer printing products and services online when paired with an e-commerce storefront. Buyers place orders on a website, portal, or an app, choosing from a catalog of products and options. They may upload existing artwork files or use an embedded online design tool to create artwork within the website.

Most systems use the order parameters to provide live estimates, accept payment, confirm the order, and move the order into the print environment. Some also pre-flight the files before confirmation to ensure the print provider can produce the job as specified. The files enter a pre-press process designed to produce the work as efficiently as possible, usually through a highly automated production workflow.

From commercial printing to books, photo books to customized apparel, home decor, promotional and gift items, and anything else that can be printed - a variety of products can be designed or customized and printed on-demand using web-to-print technology. It enables printing companies to sell and take orders online, provide live quotations, and maximize efficiencies by automating print production and faster order fulfillment. The result is stronger customer relations and an excellent customer experience.

Web-To-Print at a Glance

The global web-to-print market is constantly accelerating. The Association for Print Technologies says that it will be responsible for more than $30 billion in print sales by 2023, with two-thirds of that revenue coming from North America. Easy access to e-commerce solutions is a significant driver.

The technology makes it possible for a print buyer anywhere in the world to buy the print product they want when they want it. It democratizes print product customization when integrated with online design tools and template libraries and creates an environment conducive to exceptional print quality with integrated preflight tools.

Benefits of Implementing Web-to-Print for Customers

Consumers' increased use of the internet has enticed printers in all segments to leverage the full potential of web-to-print technology to increase their revenues. There are benefits to all parties.

A. Convenience

E-commerce printing storefronts provide potential customers access to an online catalog of products and the ability to place orders from anywhere. Whether the job is a professional business card, an invitation, marketing collateral, or a booklet, a web-to-print storefront enables non-designers to customize ready-to-use templates, choose the type of paper, and place an order conveniently - all on a single website. These storefronts often expose options for more paper and finishing options than design professionals may be aware of to enhance their projects.

B. Self-service portal for placing orders

Before the rise of web-to-print, print-ready files were traditionally delivered on a hard media like a disc or attached to an email. Online file transfer portals have also become popular. While these methods work, they disconnect the files from the order. If the client didn't have a print-ready file, they might describe the job or select from known templates and ask for it to be modified to use their color and paper choices. Again, the steps in the process can become disconnected because of the number of people and touchpoints.

Another challenge is the time it takes to get a quote and approve the final project. Web-to-print technology eliminates many of these steps, saving money and time.

Sel-service web-to-print portals allow buyers to choose pre-designed templates to personalize or upload their designs. They can preview and proofread the final design, verify it will print according to their vision, and pay for the work without external help.

Since the web-to-print storefront is a self-service portal, consumers can place orders anywhere and anytime, eliminating the need to go to a physical print store.

C. Live pricing feature

Most web-to-print solutions have an instant quotation feature that allows the buyer to choose details for their order - such as the print quantity, material type, and size of the artwork - to determine the cost for the print job. Real-time quotation saves time for both customers and print service providers.

D. Seamless payments

Did you know that 63 percent of customers exit an app or a website if they find hidden costs or cannot make payments the way they wanted to? (PayPal) The good news is that a web-to-print storefront can provide customers with a seamless and hassle-free buying experience.

Web-to-print storefronts integrated with well-designed e-commerce platforms let printers keep a tab on a customer's browsing history, including if they get stuck in the purchase cycle or simply abandon the shopping cart. Now the printer can get in touch with the customer and help them complete the process. They can also offer additional options for making payments, including cash-on-delivery (COD), debit/credit cards, net banking, PayPal, and other platforms.

E. Push notifications

Push notifications have an open rate of 90 percent. If the web-to-print solution has this feature, potential customers can receive constant updates about the status of their orders, shipping details, and delivery dates. In addition, with permission, printers can push notifications for new product launches, offers, and promotions to ensure consistent engagement with the consumers.

F. Brand consistency

Brand identity is a pivotal contributor to the success of any business. One way to create that identity is through print marketing materials such as business cards, product brochures, eBooks, and other marketing collateral. Maintaining consistency and uniformity in the use of logos, colors, and fonts across all print materials becomes more straightforward using a web-to-print software solution. They support sets of editable templates that clients can use to enforce the use of their required brand elements while allowing creativity in content customization for each project. The result is brand consistency and high-quality print.

EXERCISE #1

LIST THE POTENTIAL BENEFITS THAT WEB-TO-PRINT TECHNOLOGY CAN OFFER TO YOUR END-CUSTOMERS

1

2

3

4

5

TIP: CIRCULATE THIS SHEET AMONGST YOUR TEAM MEMBERS & ALSO ASK THEM TO ADD TO IT

Benefits of Implementing Web-to-Print for Print Service Providers

This technology is a beacon of convenience for customers. But how does it impact online printers? Let us take a look:

A. Reduced pre-production timelines and cost

Traditional print workflow, irrespective of the amount of work (250 business cards or 10,000 flyers), is time-consuming. Web-to-print technology enables a much tighter process using automation that reduces the cost of goods sold and accelerates the delivery timeline. It allows those with limited design skills to customize ready-to-print templates, saving designers for more complex projects. And, it eliminates the *price talk* making the ordering process faster and shorter, leading to more sales and more profits.

Many features, such as *placing a request for a quote*, online artwork proofing, order notifications, and easy reordering, help eliminate manual intervention and customer interaction. Staff interaction with each project becomes limited, increasing profit margins. The result is that printers have money to invest in growing sales and processing more orders per hour.

B. Eliminated artwork errors and print waste

Web-to-print storefronts allow consumers to upload their artwork, stripping away the traditional approval process, including coordination among multiple teams in the printing company. With web-to-print, even if the customer creates new artwork from scratch or uses pre-designed templates, the ball is still in their court. It is up to them to view the online design proofs and give the go-ahead. A web-to-print solution integrated with pre-flight tools and the RIP can auto-detect and notify if the artwork does not comply with the print requirements. Any mistakes in the design are caught early, reducing print errors.

Because most elements are predetermined in web-to-print software – approved artwork, print materials, colors, fonts, and finishing options - there is minimal scope for rejects or print wastage, which is a massive win for the printers.

As a result, the whole process gets shorter for both parties – all thanks to web-to-print technology. The job is reviewed, printed, and delivered faster!

C. High volume online print orders

Gone are those days when sales representatives would go from one customer to another, taking print orders. Back then, geography limited where salespeople could go, but not anymore. Today, the sky is the limit quite literally! The internet has shrunk the world.

Customers can place their orders, or the sales team can accept or create them on behalf of their customers. For consumer-facing portals, buyers place their orders from their desktop or smartphones any time of the day – all thanks to web-to-print technology. It makes taking orders smart, efficient, and profitable because printing companies can process print volumes quickly using automated systems that enable prompt deliveries.

D. Increased brand visibility by leveraging SEO

You can personalize web-to-print storefronts to your brand guidelines. Integrating it with your website theme, an intuitive user interface (UI), and user experience (UX), it will have built-in controls that maximize your content for Search Engine Optimization (SEO). You can customize the page titles, enter metadata, create keyword-rich product page URLs, and use powerful URL redirects to help prevent loss of page rank. You can get targeted visitors on your website and turn them into customers by offering them your unique services with measured digital marketing.

E. Boosted customer loyalty

There is no doubt that web-to-print technology handles multiple orders simultaneously without breaking a sweat compared to traditional methods of capturing orders and moving work into production. You can build customer loyalty and expand your share of their print buying by helping your customers configure their digital assets on your website. They will become your repeat customers and keep ordering.

With a well-configured customer environment, you can churn out orders faster and know exactly what your customer wants and when. For example, you can be the hero when your customer has an emergency order of brochures or business cards because you have all the specifications already in your system. This capability increases loyalty in your customer base and ensures a steady revenue flow.

EXERCISE #2

LIST THE POTENTIAL BENEFITS THAT WEB-TO-PRINT TECHNOLOGY CAN OFFER TO YOUR PRINTING COMPANY

1

2

3

4

5

TIP: CIRCULATE THIS SHEET AMONGST YOUR TEAM
MEMBERS & ALSO ASK THEM TO ADD TO IT

Challenges in Implementing Web-To-Print Software

Change is inevitable. But change is also often met with resistance. Many printing companies still struggle to get their customers to use their online portals. Others find that their in-house teams are resistors. So, yes. Despite significant benefits, web-to-print implementation is challenging.

Here are the challenges in greater detail in the following sections:

A. Resistance towards change

Both potential customers and employees can be hesitant when it comes to using a web-to-print solution because they are comfortable doing what they have always done and using their usual method. The resistance comes especially from those who do not understand the technology.

It is essential to convince customers that a web-to-print solution is more convenient, reduces inefficient in-house processes, and ensures a quicker turnaround time for all orders. The in-house team should be equally comfortable using the software. To help everyone, run a few training sessions to explain the nuances of web-to-print technology.

B. Lack of a skilled workforce

Lack of a skilled workforce is a global phenomenon that no printer can escape. It puts the burden on the company management to ensure that the people assigned responsibility for the operation of the storefront have the required skills and sufficient technical knowledge. Without that expertise, the web-to-print solution is at risk. You don't need software developers to run the system, but they should be people who can master the skills required to keep the system working once it is installed and activated. Work to develop proficiency in online applications and internet literacy to keep your online business channel up-to-date.

In addition, your team should be able to identify problems with the software and get them fixed. They must be able to configure the system to set for your business processes and products and services you offer online. They should be able to resolve disk space or server access issues and perform routine website management tasks with ease.

C. Initial investment and the learning curve

The implementation and rollout of a web-to-print storefront are challenging because it involves massive initial investments. Come to think of it - it is essentially an e-commerce website - selling commercial printing services to businesses and consumers.

Implementing a web-to-print storefront will not only cost you money and time but also has a steep learning curve. Once implemented, it does bring excellent value. There will be challenges, so be prepared.

D. Installation and implementation woes

A significant concern is the installation of the web-to-print software. When fully implemented, it is a direct revenue channel for your business, and you need to ensure it is up and running 24x7. The web-to-print application requires a robust server infrastructure with strong backup and security measures. Meeting this requirement can be challenging if you lack experienced IT teams to manage the servers.

In some instances, when you try to integrate two systems - for example, an MIS you are using and web-to-print software – you may experience more complexity and unprecedented delays.

The primary objective of installing web-to-print software is to ensure that the system runs smoothly, with no delays. Leverage help from your web-to-print software provider for a fail-proof implementation and ongoing maintenance.

E. Disagreements within the team

In some situations, essential management team members may fail to recognize the advantages that a print e-commerce system can bring into the business. Resolve this is by involving critical decision-makers and your unofficial leaders at the start. Be sure that they understand the benefits of the technology in terms of cost savings and faster turnaround times and how it can add value to your printing business.

It helps to develop a deck with use cases of online printing companies that have implemented web-to-print technology and flourished in their business. It may take a while for you to bring everyone up to speed; however, it is not impossible.

F. Getting customers online

Getting customers onto web-to-print storefronts is always a challenge during the initial stages due to stiff competition and diminishing customer loyalty across all print markets. You must have a marketing strategy before launching your website in the market.

Make it as easy as possible. Write a series of tutorials and video guides giving a step-by-step process of navigating through the storefront with ease. Create a quarterly campaign for promoting your website - promoting its benefits and how convenient the technology makes the buying process.

Additionally, you can conduct user tests to understand your potential customers' likes and dislikes about the storefront before going live with the final product. We discuss this in greater detail later in the book.

G. Persistent usage

Another major challenge printing companies face is persuading their customers (and staff) to use the web-to-print software consistently.

Traditionally, printing deals with massive paperwork and offline tasks. A web-to-print solution helps you and your customers make the transition with a more digital approach. Help them understand the process of using the software to create the infrastructure for success. Once your customers recognize the benefits, they are more likely to use the solution regularly.

H. Maintenance and upgrades

Periodic software upgrades enhance system performance and speed. The in-house team must maintain and upgrade the web-to-print software regularly. Delaying upgrades can bring your website to a halt, hampering the buying experience for your potential customers.

It is vital that your in-house team regularly communicates with the IT department and uses their help to fix impending software issues if the need arises. Investing in maintenance contracts is a best practice to ensure that your web-to-print storefront features always function optimally.

EXERCISE #3

LIST THE CHALLENGES THAT WEB-TO-PRINT TECHNOLOGY CAN POSE FOR YOUR END-CUSTOMERS AND YOUR IN-HOUSE TEAM

1

2

3

4

5

TIP: CIRCULATE THIS SHEET AMONGST YOUR TEAM MEMBERS & ALSO ASK THEM TO ADD TO IT

Verticals where Web-to-Print has Proven Results

The global commercial print market remains in a constant state of transition. Significant business growth opportunities for printing companies are still on the rise.

Rampant advancements in technology, particularly web-to-print technology, simplify the print buying process. Today any consumer can personalize items and place orders in minutes. On top of that, online printing companies can offer a broader range of products, collaborate with consumers more efficiently, and produce printed orders faster.

It doesn't matter if you sell custom-decorated apparel, personalized packaging, or ready-for-print drinkware. There is potential in every domain, waiting to be tapped by printing companies that adopt web-to-print technology.

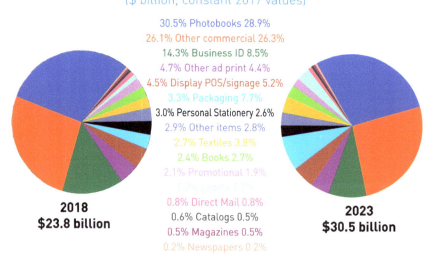

Developing product mix of web-to-print output, 2018 and 2023
($ billion, constant 2017 values)

30.5% Photobooks 28.9%
26.1% Other commercial 26.3%
14.3% Business ID 8.5%
4.7% Other ad print 4.4%
4.5% Display POS/signage 5.2%
3.3% Packaging 7.7%
3.0% Personal Stationery 2.6%
2.9% Other items 2.8%
2.7% Textiles 3.8%
2.4% Books 2.7%
2.1% Promotional 1.9%
1.2% Labels 2.3%
0.8% Direct Mail 0.8%
0.6% Catalogs 0.5%
0.5% Magazines 0.5%
0.2% Newspapers 0.2%

2018
$23.8 billion

2023
$30.5 billion

The good news is that web-to-print is not restricted to only one industry. It has spread its branches across the print market. This section gives you an overview of all of them:

A. Commercial printing

Commercial printing covers many varieties. The process involves transferring artwork onto a substrate, like paper or card stock. The rise of e-commerce has transformed it, allowing printers to serve customers anywhere in the world using web-to-print technology paired with online payment solutions.

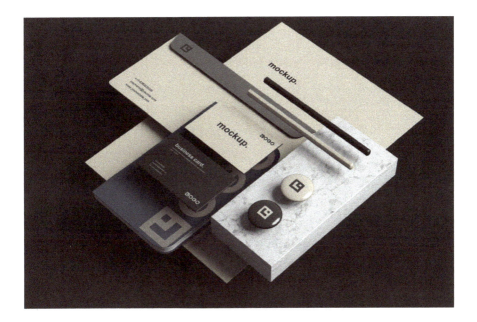

B. In-plant printing

In-plant printers are not commercial printers; instead, they function like any department in an organization, such as human resources, marketing, finance, or operations. They are prevalent in colleges, universities, government offices, banks, insurance companies, enterprise campuses, and other institutions with significant internal printing requirements.

In-plant printers typically face different types of challenges from commercial printers, including limited budgets and workforce allocation, accessibility, managing urgent requirements, security challenges, timely access to data for variable data work, and internal approval processes. Web-to-print technology brings efficiency by allowing individual departments to upload their print jobs for processing, reprint previous orders, create customized designs on approved templates, and order items from inventory for printing with ease.

C. Wide-format printing

One of the most lucrative markets in the digital print industry, wide-format printing supports sign and large format print for many applications. More applications regularly emerge as new substrates, inks, and marking technologies develop, leading to new opportunities. Online printers are adding banners, soft signage, packaging, printeriors, and fabric printing.

D. Decorated apparel

The average apparel order size is increasing, and social media has proven a robust means of attracting a more extensive customer base and generating new leads. The desire for logo apparel is strong, especially in the B2B spectrum. [Advertising Speciality Institute] The global decorated apparel market is likely to continue growing, according to most industry research. Embroidery, screen printing, patches/emblems, vinyl letters design, and head transfers are five of the services, along with Web-To-Print technology driving market growth.

E. Promotional and personalized gifting

As an evolving industry, promotional gifts have shifted from picture frames and coffee mugs to highly personalized items with creative and innovative packaging, monogram engravings, and personalized notes.

F. Digital fabrics

Smithers Pira expects the digital fabric print industry to continue to grow. Most other market researchers agree. It's not surprising that the digital fabrics industry has grown exponentially as new printing techniques such as screen printing and direct to garment (DTG) continue to expand. The online t-shirt printing business is one example. Not only are the t-shirts cheap to source and simple to customize, but the global market for these personalized items grows each year.

But that is not all. Web-to-print technology enables platforms for digital printing fabrics for a variety of applications. More than just printing on t-shirts, today, companies can digitally print custom bolts of fabric for home décor and fashion.

G. Custom box and packaging

Many studies show how important packaging is to customer perception of the products they contain. Brands can promote their offerings and even change their image with packaging.

Licious.in is an India-based poultry company and online seller of meat and seafood. It does a great job with its packaging, using caricatures of its customers on the delivery boxes. No wonder Licious.in always receives positive feedback for its unique packaging initiatives.

If you check their social media channels, you will find that their customers have posted pictures of the boxes on delivery. That social amplification automatically raises the bar for Liscious.in as a brand.

A significant perk of selling custom packaging services is that it enables clients to design what they need to best fit the product. They may want to add corner pieces that keep the fragile products in place or other types of packaging inserts. Web-to-print technology offers this functionality.

H. Printeriors

Printerior options result from substrate manufacturers and digital printers joining to showcase a new range of applications targeted at interior design communities. That opened the doors to new creative possibilities enabling innovative interior design concepts across multiple domains such as commercial and residential real estate, retail, and hospitality.

You might find it anywhere because the technology can print on metal, wood, composites, glass, ceramic tiles, and Perspex. The reach has expanded, with designers leveraging the advances in digital textile printing to develop on-demand bespoke cushions, furniture upholstery, carpets, table covers, drapes, and more – without requirements for minimum order sizes. Room interiors in some European and American hotels are now entirely digitally printed.

This is an excellent opportunity for online printing businesses to leverage web-to-print technology and offer consumers options to design and buy personalized home decor. Thanks to the web-to-print business model, online printers don't have to keep a large stock of pre-printed materials. They can order what they need when there is demand, saving costs and reducing wastage.

I. Photo books and booklets

Photo books increase in popularity and options every year, enabled by web-to-print technology. Most photobooks are designed and executed through web-to-print portals, which now offer everything from budget options to high-end luxury finishes.

J. Drinkware

Drinkware such as tumblers, mugs, glassware, and ceramics are huge e-commerce commodities. An increasing number of consumers are *going green* and opting for eco-friendly and personalized options. The industry meets these demands with the help of web-to-print technology that makes personalizing beverage items possible - for instance, adding a company logo or a photograph on a coffee mug and using specific colors for its design.

K. Labels and stickers

This industry thrives on personalization. Given the ever-increasing demand for more creative and innovative ideas, web-to-print technology enables businesses and consumers to design product labels, photo labels, barcode labels, asset labels, packaging labels, and mailing labels. Customizable templates make it easier for new customers to create what they need and ensure it can be printed as desired.

This segment is especially attractive for web-to-print technology, which enables growth. After all, who doesn't love to have the freedom to alter the sizes and shapes of their labels and stickers and choose appropriate materials for their project?

Success Stories

In an age of rampant digital technological advancements, where every business is looking to carve a niche for themselves, web-to-print technology has empowered the print industry. It enables printing businesses to leverage the inherent potential of the World Wide Web by allowing them to think beyond merely *offering print services*.

If there is one thing that our experience as a leading web-to-print software provider has taught us, this technology can do wonders for your business. Today, online printers can not only reach a more extensive consumer base and expand their service offerings but also offer their target customers an optimal shopping experience, which was tricky until a few years ago. No wonder an increasing number of printing businesses are deploying web-to-print technology in their existing operational workflows.

Below are five compelling industry use cases of printing companies that transformed into growth machines thanks to web-to-print.

A. FASteambanners

W2P benefit: Advanced design template editing features for team banners. Before the US-based online printer switched to web-to-print, FASteambanners had a simple website with a Flash-based design tool. Due to the limited functionality, their customers could not change colors of clipart or use advanced design template editing features. Once an order was placed online, the back office production team of FASteambanners could not edit customer-designed signs after downloading their created file. These challenges led to a thinning customer base, high turnaround time, and a limited product catalog.

With web-to-print technology, they overhauled their website design, added a non-flash HTML5 design tool plus a support staff that understood their website and business inside out.

B. SilkLetter

W2P benefit: A B2B personalized shopping experience

Since its inception in 2008, SilkLetter, a New York-based B2B promotional product and corporate gifting printer, struggled to flourish. The biggest reason was that they did not offer personalization to the customer base. After an exhaustive search, they realized they needed a web-to-print solution customized to their industry requirements and not merely a plug-and-play solution that most vendors in the market provided.

When SilkLetter joined hands with their chosen web-to-print vendor, they spent months outlining the scope of work demanded by their niche and taking actions to mitigate any future risks. SilkLetter has not reported a single website downtime since they changed solutions, and their sales have increased.

It is not a surprise that leveraging web-to-print technology in business processes has significantly benefited the printing companies.

Find Your Why

Investing in web-to-print technology is like outsourcing. You outsource menial tasks such as sharing quotes, taking orders, getting artwork approval, and following up on payments. With the help of technology, your in-house team is freed from other tasks, and they can offer additional high-end services such as on-demand marketing, web development, IT services, and more – all in the realm of printing.

Branching out can double or triple your annual sales and increase your ROI. You can tap new opportunities and ensure multiple incomes, rather than just focusing on one offering or service, which most businesses do.

Now that you know the benefits you can reap from web-to-print technology, have you established the goals you would like to achieve with it? Is it to increase leads, increase conversions through sign-ups or subscriptions, grow in brand interactions, or improve customer service?

Whatever your goals are, this technology can do wonders for your business and boost your ROI.

EXERCISE #4

PUT ON YOUR THINKING CAP AND WRITE 5-6 REASONS WHY WEB-TO-PRINT IS WHAT YOU NEED FOR YOUR ONLINE PRINTING BUSINESS:

1

2

3

4

5

TIP: CIRCULATE THIS SHEET AMONGST YOUR TEAM MEMBERS & ALSO ASK THEM TO ADD TO IT

ROI Calculator

Many online printing companies like yours that purchase web-to-print software often fail to implement it properly. When that happens, the idea to leverage the technology is never fulfilled. Since web-to-print is the present and future of the print market, extra precautions are warranted to avoid being a repeat web-to-print guinea pig. Take steps to do it right this time.

The first step is to calculate the finances. Web-to-print technology is a considerable investment, and we can imagine how you would feel if you failed to tap into its potential. We honestly would not recommend it to any online printer if you are unsure about your investment return.

Since you are a business owner, we know it is all about the numbers, so we introduce this compelling ROI calculator.

It works for both existing businesses and startups. By answering the short questionnaire and using the formula shared below, you can estimate your cost savings in time taken to send the artwork for approval, process an order, fulfill shipment, and calculate your return on investment. It is worth a try, especially when you are confused about incorporating new technology to boost your revenues.

ENTER VALUES

A	How many orders do you receive every day? (e.g., 5, 10, 15)	
B	How many orders do you receive from new customers every day? (e.g., 5, 10, 15)	
C	How many orders do you receive from your repeat customers every day? (e.g.,5, 10, 15)	
D	Please enter the average order value. (e.g., 10, 20, 30 USD)	
E	Please enter the profit margin of your business (e.g., 5 percent, 10 percent, 15 percent)	
F	Please enter the hourly labor rate (e.g., $20 per hour)	
G	Please enter the number of working days in a month (e.g. 20,22,25)	

CONSIDERATIONS

Web-to-print technology saves 30 minutes on every order you take by phone/email. Here is the breakdown:

The order received from the customer enters into the system (10 mins)
Proofing: The customer is sent proof of the job for approval (10 min)
Job queuing: Your team enters the job in queue for printing (5 mins)
Status update: The customer is informed of the order status & delivery (5 mins)

[J] We observe a 30% revenue hike from a new customer after deploying web-to-print technology.

[K] We see a 40% revenue hike from existing customers after using web-to-print technology.

RETURN ON INVESTMENT CALCULATIONS

H	**Labor cost saved per order** = 30/60 (30 mins saved on every order)* Labor hourly rate [F]	
I	**Monthly labor cost saved** Labor cost saved per order [H]* Total number of orders per day [A]* Number of working days [G]	
M	**Total number of order hikes from new customers in a month** = Orders you receive from new customers every day [B] * [K]/100 * Number of working days [G]	
N	**Total revenue hikes from new customers in a month** = Total number of orders hikes from new customers in a month [M] * Average order value [D]	
O	**Monthly profit growth from new customers** = Total revenue hikes from new customers in a month [N]* Profit margin of your business [E]	
P	**Total number of order hikes from existing customers in a month** = Orders you receive from your repeat customers every day [C]* [L]/100 * Number of working days [G]	
Q	**Total revenue hikes from existing customers in a month** =Total number of order hikes from existing customers in a month [P] * Average order value [D]	
R	**Monthly profit growth from existing customers** =Total revenue hikes from existing customers in a month [Q]* Profit margin of your business [E]	
S	**Monthly profit after implementing web-to-print** = Monthly labor cost saved [I]+ Monthly profit growth from new customers [O]+ Monthly profit growth from existing customers [R]	
T	**Yearly profit after implementing web-to-print** = Monthly profit after implementing webtoprint [S] * 12 months	

Access Design'N'Buy's FREE digital calculator on:
https://www.designnbuy.com/ROI-calculator-printers

PROJECT
PLANNING PHASE

It is okay for you to break into a cold sweat at the very thought of web-to-print software implementation. Embarking on something that has the potential to boost your workflow efficiency, increase sales by 58 percent (Epicomm), and disrupt the customer experience can do that to you.

Benjamin Franklin once said, "By failing to prepare, you are preparing to fail." Successful implementation of your web-to-print software lies in a solid base for the project and nailing down the details. But if you don't have a team that knows what they are supposed to do, failure is inevitable.

A web-to-print software implementation is a substantial investment, which affects teams across verticals - from operations to marketing. That's why you need to make sure you have a member from each business function to do their part of the job, which is tied to your web-to-print software implementation outcome.

Great teams don't just deliver results; they are committed to the project. And in this case, it is your responsibility to set up such a team.

In the following section, we will discuss some success-boosting tips vital to the project planning phase:

The Project Planning Phase

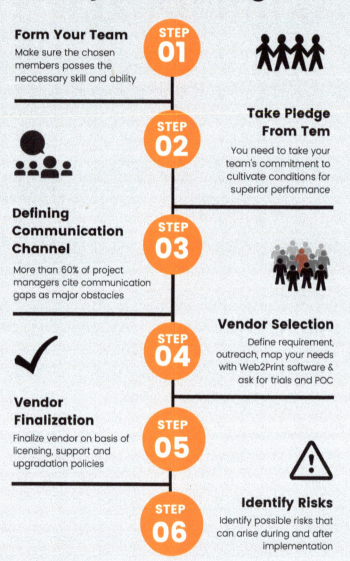

Form Your Team
Make sure the chosen members posses the neccessary skill and ability

STEP 01

STEP 02

Take Pledge From Tem
You need to take your team's commitment to cultivate conditions for superior performance

Defining Communication Channel
More than 60% of project managers cite communication gaps as major obstacles

STEP 03

STEP 04

Vendor Selection
Define requirement, outreach, map your needs with Web2Print software & ask for trials and POC

Vendor Finalization
Finalize vendor on basis of licensing, support and upgradation policies

STEP 05

STEP 06

Identify Risks
Identify possible risks that can arise during and after implementation

Benjamin Franklin once said "By failing to prepare, you're preparing to fail "

Form Your Team

"Who is doing what?" or "We don't know where to begin" is not something you want to hear from anyone in your company at the start of the web-to-print software implementation. To avoid this scenario, the first and most crucial step is to get everyone on the same page and explain how your company can benefit from the web-to-print software.

Begin with a discussion of the *Key Performance Indicators* (KPIs) you are tracking and how they relate to everyone's responsibilities. Make sure they know how their contributions affect the implementation.

Once you have conducted due diligence for the proposed plan and given inputs to everyone in the company, form a team that will help you successfully implement the web-to-print software. Keep the following points in mind:

1. Ensure the team you select has the necessary skills and abilities required for the job. They don't need to be qualified in absolute terms, but they should be the most qualified for your specific project.

2. Select a mix of team members - each with a different set of core skills and abilities - rather than a series of clones with identical qualities.

3. Make sure your team represents all the skills you need in the proportions required.

4. Don't overlook the need to choose people who can get along with one another and work productively as a team. Conflicts are bound to arise in a project when camaraderie amongst team members is not considered.

EXERCISE #5

We are sure you have specific employees in mind, from different departments, whom you would like to be a part of the implementation. In the worksheet below, put their names against each department and mention their responsibilities:

DEPARTMENT	TEAM MEMBERS	RESPONSIBILITIES
PROJECT OWNER		
IT		
FINANCE		
ACCOUNTING		
ART/GRAPHICS		
PRE-PRESS		
ORDER MANAGEMENT		
SHIPPING/ FULFILLMENT		
OPERATIONS		
MARKETING/ BRANDING		
SALES		

TIP: ADD THIS SHEET TO THE PROJECT BRIEF AT THE START OF THE IMPLEMENTATION SO THAT EVERY TEAM MEMBER KNOWS WHO OWNS WHICH PARTS OF THE PROJECT AND WHOM TO CONTACT IN TIMES OF NEED.

Qualities of a Successful Project Team

Setting up a team is fun, tiresome, and even complicated. But with the right direction, it is often the most exciting part of the project. Here are six qualities to look for in your team:

A. Strong leadership

To make the implementation phase a success, you need to appoint someone who can lead the team. That person should be able to communicate the project objectives and vision to the team, delegate tasks, and manage team members - with the utmost professionalism. John Maxwell said, "A leader is one who knows the way, goes the way, and shows the way." Our years of implementation experience have taught us that the teams led by influential leaders are the most successful ones. You need to find a strong leader who can successfully drive the web-to-print software implementation.

B. Diligent execution

An Executor is someone who understands the relevant requirements of the job and has a strong desire and ability to get the job done. Web-to-print software implementations are not plug and play and can be prone to problems and delays.

That is why each aspect of the implementation phase must be monitored and regulated. The Executor should be in charge of cost management, delivery timelines, and evaluating potential risks involved in the project.

They should be responsible for controlling the schedule, allocating resources, and setting realistic deadlines while identifying potential risks and their impacts. It is also essential to make plans to mitigate problems that arise.

C. Collaboration

When team members work together collaboratively and understand each other's strengths and weaknesses, they can balance the work. They can also make decisions based on feedback and knowledge gathered from all the team members rather than a single individual.

Giving your team sufficient authority to make changes required to overcome barriers to flow will help them work more efficiently and productively. They will also feel more confident about themselves.

D. Tech-savviness

Your team should have a firm grasp of the web-based application, technologies involved in its development, and the implementation lifecycle. There will be technical talks, so they should be able to absorb the information and share it across the company in succinct terms.

The skill index of the team members should also be taken into consideration so that they can constructively contribute to the project's technical requirements.

E. Clear communication

It turns out that when wise people say, "Communication is the simplest solution to most of our problems," they are right. Research proves that face-to-face interactions among team members can boost the team's performance by 35 percent. (HBR) Successful teams consist of people that are open to feedback and the opinions of each other and work together to develop ideas and solutions for the project.

It helps to create an environment that makes it easier to resolve conflicts of opinions or a disagreement of ideas. The best teams communicate with each other and make decisions without hampering the progress of the W2P implementation.

F. Enthusiasm

In our experience, enthusiasm is one trait that can fetch optimistic results for any project. It helps when a team works towards a common goal, shares similar levels of commitment to the job, celebrates all wins, and acknowledges and rectifies mistakes.

If your team members are excited to work together and are fully invested in the progress of the web-to-print software implementation, the chances of it becoming hugely successful increase automatically.

Tip: *Before you start the implementation phase, arrange to have a demo of your web-to-print software to clarify their doubts (if they have any) to ensure they are committed to the goal and enthusiastic about making the project work.*

EXERCISE #6

Before you finalize the team members and set up the team, conduct a brief discussion with each selected individual to understand how committed he/she is to be a part of this project. After all you want enthusiastic and self-driven people to work with you!

This may seem like project management 101, but the checklist below will make sure your new team members are aligned to the goal of the project.

- Does every member of the team have a clear understanding of what the company is trying to achieve with the W2P implementation?

- Does every member of the team understand how his/her piece of the project ties back to the overall outcome? Get each individual to affirm the understanding in writing.

- Have you appointed the project leader as a first step? Is he qualified for the role and have relevant experience in implementing a software application? Set out his role and responsibilities very clearly before you do it for each member of the web-to-print implementation team.

- Derive an effective communication plan so that all team members meet regularly and stick to the objective of the project throughout the implementation phase.

Project Team Pledge

To cultivate the conditions for superior performance in your team, you need to reinforce a positive mindset. The 7-point pledge shared below lays out clear and concise rules for your team to follow:

PROJECT TEAM PLEDGE

▶ Set out a detailed implementation program and stick to it

▶ Agree on targets and milestones, and identify what needs to be done and by when

▶ Update the tasks completed on the project management softeare provided

▶ Work closely with the W2P solution provider to finish the implementation phase faster

▶ Obtain data on performance and results, and use and share this learning to drive continued progress

▶ Communicate whenever there is a problem

▶ Embrace change with open-mindedness

Tip: If you want your team members to anchor these promises in their beliefs, they need to read them as often as they can. Post copies of the pledge throughout the workplace so that it stays visible.

Defining a Communication Channel for the Team

Almost 60 percent of project managers find the lack of communication the biggest obstacle to business success. (Atlassian)

This section explains what it takes to create a transparent communication process for your team.

A. Communicate the project clearly

There are many project planning and implementation methods. Whichever you select should accommodate a project kick-off to explain the plan and answer questions. During the project, there should be regular meetings. One type is a sprint meeting where progress is noted and the following milestones are set. Think about adding specific meetings to resolve problems and let team members ask questions. You might have short sprint meetings weekly and a more extended Q&A session monthly.

Remember to address progress on the project and address any bottlenecks hampering the deliverability. To ensure your team stays well-connected, deploy collaboration tools such as Skype, Slack, What's App, Microsoft Teams, Zoom, or GoToMeeting for distributed teams and remote workers.

B. Define the resources needed

Allocate a budget for acquiring or developing the solution. The best practice is to include:

- Cost and timeline of buying or building the web-to-print software
- The hosting fee for the server to run the application
- The price of acquiring your domain and SSL
- Preparing the content for your website

- Populating your storefront with products and completing all configurations
- Your unique design templates that your customers can personalize and order
- Testing and verifying the end-to-end buying process
- Setting up a merchant account with payment and shipping gateways
- Setting a marketing and branding budget to promote your website to boost your search engine rankings
- The burdened cost of the in-house implementation team.

Projects fail when the decision-makers don't consider some of these costs in their initial business plan and are unprepared to conquer financial hurdles.

C. Draft your requirement for the project

Choose what products you want to offer to your customers online. Prepare a step-by-step plan and do not try to do everything at once. It is better to segment your priorities into implementation phases, tackling them one by one.

For example, you can start with an essential website, listing products that consumers often buy online and letting them send you requests for quotes. This way, you can understand the interest of your potential customers to purchase from you online.

Later, you can add features to let them upload their artwork and place orders with instant payments. Finally, you can let them customize your product templates or create a new one with the help of an easy-to-use design studio within your website to produce print-ready files that are ready to order.

A phased implementation always helps to deal with one goal at a time and ensure a smooth client onboarding.

D. Define the timelines and prioritize

For any team to breeze through deadlines requires them to prioritize tasks. Your team members should break down every task into smaller, achievable deadlines that can be tracked. It is better to finish a project as big as web-to-print implementation in smaller steps that allow for incremental adjustment rather than working on larger pieces that may require rework because they were not aligned with the business strategy or because they were filled with errors.

Attainable goals are the core of project management. Ensure that the implementation phase of your web-to-print software is divided so that your teams can make progress every day. Completion of smaller tasks will also help boost their morale.

EXERCISE #7

Think about the last three projects you have been a part of that did not go well because of poor communication. Now list different ways to streamline the communication during the implementation phase:

- Decide what form of communication works best for your team and identify the centralized communication tool that your team will use throughout the implementation.

- Define a regular meeting schedule to track the progress, and identify the key artifacts that each team member should prepare for the meeting.

- What will be the acceptable response time for each team member for any form of requested communication?

4. Identify a feedback system for team member to post their suggestions and feedback.

TIP: TO MAKE THINGS INTERESTING, PRINT THIS PAGE OUT AND ASK OTHER PEOPLE WHO WORKED ON THOSE PROJECTS TO FILL IT OUT, TOO – THEN COMPARE NOTES

Vendor Selection

Any online printing company will agree that to ensure significant business growth in the future; they must have a strong IT support team to meet the needs of their ever-demanding customers. It is the essential requirement of running a successful online business. Choosing a web-to-print software provider is another responsibility you cannot take lightly.

In this section, we will discuss four major factors to consider when choosing a web-to-print solution for your online printing business:

A. Map your business requirements

In 2019, Design'N'Buy surveyed a mix of 455 online printers over three months to understand their main reasons for implementing web-to-print technology. From the responses received, three objectives stood out:

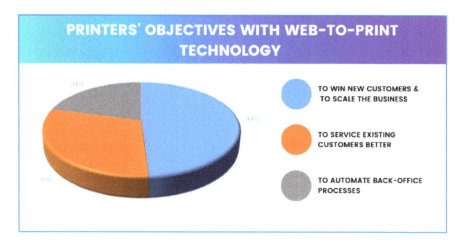

Therefore, the first step is to define the business objectives that your online printing company wants to achieve with web-to-print technology. These objectives could include streamlining business operations or expanding product offerings, increasing market reach, further developing your reseller network, or improving customer retention.

Web-to-print technology is a growth enabler for online printers because it helps them make sales 24/7 and provide their customers with a better buying experience by being a one-stop solution for all printing needs. If you can narrow your current and future business objectives, whatever they may be, you can successfully choose the right web-to-print vendor for your company and fulfill those objectives.

B. Define vendor selection criteria

Many software vendors sell web-to-print solutions. However, depending on how sophisticated the platform is, there may be significant expenses associated with setting up a storefront and working through the back-end processes. The investment is enormous, and you can't afford to spend time on demos, finalizing a vendor, and deploying the software - only to realize that the product won't help you achieve your business objectives.

Therefore, to make things easier, here are 18 elements to look for in web-to-print software:

a. Customizations and scalability

Each online printer has its array of printing machinery. Each has a set print method and file format specification, pricing logic, product catalog, and business requirements. The web-to-print software should cater to all those needs to avoid running multiple systems simultaneously.

For example, printer A could specialize in selling t-shirts but wants to offer customizable stationery. A web-to-print system that permits selling both online will be the right choice. The solution should be fully customizable and easily scalable so that new products and features can be added later, as needed. The solution should also be able to scale as the online business grows.

b. **Language and currency localization**

If the business plans to cater to customers from multiple countries, language localization is a valuable option for web-to-print software. It also helps to support multiple currencies and payment methods so that consumers can make purchases from anywhere in the world.

c. **API availability for third-party software integration**

Your web-to-print software should have a robust and scalable architecture that makes it easy to integrate it with any third-party application and even your in-house solutions for seamless online business automation. This could include preflight tools, RIP software, Customer Relationship Management (CRM), Enterprise Resource Planning (ERP), accounting software, an inventory management system, cloud storage, image library tools, and similar solutions.

d. **Cross-browser and platform readiness**

The solution should be compatible with all modern browsers and operating systems so that your customers can shop on your website from anywhere at any time, including browsing and ordering through smartphones and tablets. Enable them to access the website and customize their orders without downloading a mobile app. It makes their buying experience stress-free!

e. **SEO optimization**

Your web-to-print software should feature a URL that is friendly to Search Engine Optimization (SEO) and comes with its suite of SEO tools to make it easy for your storefront to rank high in search results. It should also have a responsive storefront design and high-quality user experience to encourage longer browsing sessions, boosting search rankings.

f. Application security

The frequency of cyber-attacks has increased manifold. What is scarier is the sophistication of this warfare. Phishing, malware, ransomware, e-skimming, cross-site scripting, and SQL injection are a few conventional cyber-attack methods. The current state has given birth to security measures to protect online businesses and their customers against all forms of cyber threats, including:

- Implementing strong, unique passwords (at least eight characters with upper and lowercase letters, special characters, and numbers) and advising all consumers to follow the practice.

- Never revealing personal information to any recipient via email or clicking suspicious email links, and advising all consumers to avoid falling into such phishing traps.

- Implementing a 2-step authentication to assure that only the authorized users are logging into the web-to-print storefront.

- Ensuring the web-to-print storefront is secure with anti-virus software, firewalls, or any other appropriate method of protecting against any cyber threats.

- Only storing consumer data that you need to conduct business, and only as long as you need it.

- Opting for secure HTTPS hosting that requires an SSL certificate will help you secure your web-to-print storefront.

- Regularly reviewing all third-party integrations and plugins used on the storefront.

- Keeping security patches up to date.

Therefore, the chosen web-to-print software solution should offer security at both website and server levels to protect your customer data regardless of who has access. The best W2P solutions offer military-grade encryptions for complete security and protection against unauthorized data access and multiple threats and vulnerabilities related to online commerce.

g. Upselling and cross-selling

Your web-to-print software should have a flexible catalog management system that incorporates cross-selling and upselling on product pages. This will help you increase the average order value (AOV) by encouraging your existing and potential customers to buy more.

Product recommendations are a big thing in e-commerce. Sessions without any engagement or recommendations have an AOV of only $44.41. However, this number multiplies by 369 percent when consumers engage with a single recommendation. [Barilliance]

h. Multi-vendor compatibility

A significant advantage of setting up your online store is that you can list and sell products that you do not print in-house. You can outsource to third-party vendors based on a pre-set commission and offer a one-stop online portal to your customers. The web-to-print software solution should allow you to automatically add multiple vendors and outsource projects from the back-end without manual intervention.

After all - it would be best if you had complete control over role-based access of the system for your vendors/sellers. There should also be a central administration analytics feature to track each vendor's performance so that improvements can be identified and executed.

i. Payment gateway support

Did you know 56 percent of consumers expect a variety of payment options on the checkout page? (Milo)

Lack of options either puts them off entirely or triggers them to abandon the store without completing the purchase. Both scenarios are detrimental to the company's sales.

Your web-to-print software should be compatible with multiple payment gateway options, including popular payment methods such as PayPal, GooglePay, and Amazon Pay so that your customers around the world can use their preferred payment option.

j. Shipping integration

Shipping options should be easy to integrate into the web-to-print software, including real-time tracking and carrier rates display. You should have the opportunity to display account-specific, flat, or table rates depending on the business model used.

Many web-to-print storefronts partner with shipping vendors so that the end customer can see the exact status of the delivery on the website itself. USPS, FedEx, DHL, and UPS are some well-known carriers.

Note that the capability differs from vendor to vendor in the web-to-print industry. Most of the time, the end client is taken to the shipping vendor's website for tracking purposes. But some web-to-print storefronts update the order status on their system itself, making it easier for the end client to know the status without going to a third-party website.

k. Print-ready output file format and compatibility with your production process

The print-ready files offered by the web-to-print software come in file formats compatible with your machines. This is critical to ensure that the printed versions of your items are in high resolution and in the right size to avoid any manual adjustments before sending them to the printing press.

l. Number of design templates and the ability to create your library

It will help if you verify that the templates and designs can be uploaded in a compatible format to save rework. Also, there should be a template builder so that your graphics team can set up a fresh batch of templates as required.

The best practice is for the web-to-print solution to offer a set of pre-loaded, editable design templates to suit different needs. This will reduce your go-live efforts.

m. Support for pricing setup

The solution should allow complete flexibility to set up and modify product prices as needed. The storefront should automatically reflect pricing based on buying options chosen by the customer, such as tier pricing, discounts, or limited-period sales, as well as coupon codes that an individual customer may be using.

n. Timeline and project execution process

The solution should include a print workflow management system so that your team can keep track of the status of each order until it is completed, shipped, and delivered. Also, as each printing product can have a different processing workflow, the web-to-print solution should allow you to set up a product-specific print workflow. There should also be a provision for your customers to check their orders' delivery status.

o. **Reporting and status update strategy**

Your web-to-print software should offer access to a variety of reports that provide detailed updates on how the store is performing. This will enable you to make actionable changes (i.e., fix any glitches or upgrade whenever) to improve customer experience and retention.

p. **Service level agreement**

The web-to-print software provider should offer a comprehensive service level agreement (SLA) that lays out the exact responsibilities, metrics, and expectations that you can expect in the contract. The agreement should also include details on the steps to be taken if issues arise with either party.

q. **Single point of contact**

There should be a single point of contact for you to reach out to in case of any disputes or support requirements. The POC from the web-to-print software provider should be reachable over phone, text, email, and fax and respond promptly and accurately to any questions.

r. **Customer accounts**

Your customers should have the ability to save items to a wish list and share their artwork with friends and family over social media accounts. They should be able to access and update their contact information, submit ratings and reviews, manage their photos and digital assets online, so they don't need to be re-uploaded every time they wish to place an order.

If the web-to-print software solution allows them to save their designs, access it later, and then order upon finish, that is an added advantage in customer service. The better the customer experience, the higher are the chances of quick adoption of your online channel for order acquisition.

s. **Blog and CMS**

Your web-to-print software should have a built-in blog system and CMS to create pages with images, video, and dynamic content and modify existing pages, blocks, and widgets. Since blogging is a big part of digital marketing, you must ensure that the feature is up-to-mark.

C. Vendor outreach, communication, and initial demo

The web-to-print software provider should be proactive and helpful when reaching out to you and communicating effectively about the technology. You should have the option of requesting a personalized demo and/or scheduling a personal consultation session where you can get an in-depth understanding of solution features, implementation cycle, pricing models, and other vital details before you discuss with your team and take a call.

D. Trial with sample products setup and print runs with output files

The web-to-print provider should offer you a free demo, including sample products setup on the storefront, testing of the design editor tools, and sample print runs with output files in multiple formats for ensuring its viability for your business. This will also allow you to determine whether the solution offers the desired level of flexibility and whether the final output is compatible with your equipment and production standards. If the web-to-print software provider can show you exactly how much value is being created for you with the technology, then, by all means, strike a deal with them.

EXERCISE #8

Use the space below to chart the "current state" and "ideal state" of your business process and production workflow, and highlight the significant objectives you want to achieve and/or issues you want to eliminate with the new solution:

CURRENT STATE MAP
A process flowchart showing the current state of production workflow.

IDEAL STATE MAP
A process flowchart highlighting what would be your ideal production workflow for online orders.

OBJECTIVES/ISSUES
Objectives you want to achieve and Issues you want to eliminate.

TIP: INVOLVE ALL THE TEAMS THAT WILL USE THE WEB-TO-PRINT SOFTWARE SOLUTION, AND GET INPUTS FROM EVERYONE INVOLVED. CLEAR COMMUNICATION IS KEY!

Vendor Finalization

The evolution of the online print industry is nothing less than a marvel. Consumers today are no longer dependent on brick-and-mortar stores to get something printed. Thanks to digitalization, printing services are now available online, around the clock - offering benefits to consumers and online printing companies like yours.

It can be overwhelming to find a web-to-print software provider. Adopting and deploying new technology for the betterment of your storefront is serious business. The stakes of collaborating with a suitable vendor are high for you. But, if you have decided to implement the technology, half the battle is won. All you need to do is research web-to-print software providers extensively and talk to as many of them as possible, asking them relevant questions, as shared below:

A. What does your software license policy entail? Will I have control over my license?

Never underestimate the value of owning your software license. Check if it is perpetual or time-bound. If it is time-bound, ask for the renewal policy and the fees involved.

It is also essential that you should be able to customize your website with your brand colors and logo. However, if you cannot make such adjustments to the software on your own, the process of implementation can be tedious.

You will be required to coordinate with your web-to-print vendor for every small cosmetic change on your website to reflect your brand identity.

Many web-to-print software providers will guarantee that you are entirely in charge of the system. However, certain areas of the application may be closed source codes, and you may be required to reach out to their support team to initiate customizations.

So make sure that you check open-source code availability for certain features of the application that need frequent updates.

This includes updating website branding elements, updating product pricing or sizes, adding new products and design templates to the catalog, integrating a new payment gateway, and more. Therefore, always confirm the flexibility you will get using web-to-print software.

B. Can you please elaborate on your business models (on-premises or SaaS) and payment terms?

When it comes to investing significantly in technology, every business needs flexibility in payments. Ask the chosen vendor about the types of business models they offer and choose the one that suits you the best. The most common are owning the perpetual license for the software or renting it on a software-as-a-subscription (SaaS) basis.

Choose the right model based on your budget, expected timeline for implementation, internal team availability, skills to operate the online website, ability to customize the solution per your business needs, and other essential aspects.

License vs. SaaS

LICENSE VS SAAS

LICENSE	SAAS
You own the software even though the upfront costs are high	You own the software even though the upfront costs are high
Can be used for as long as you want	Can be used for as long as you keep renewing the subscription
New hardware, cloud servers or software may be required	No need for hardware or software as it is hosted by the vendor
Can also run on separate offline or intranet systems	Can only be used with internet access
Total ownership cost is less after 3-4 years	Total cost of ownership may be higher after a few years
Full control when service goes down	No control when service goes down

Many software companies also offer a Free Trial before you purchase it. Take advantage of that and test the solution with real-time scenarios to ensure you invest in the real deal to set up your online print business. Cross-check if there are any additional fees beyond the license or subscription fees, such as setup, transaction, currency exchange, or maintenance fees. Ask them about their deployment process and if there is any added cost to run the application successfully.

Confirm what happens when your website goes over specific quotas or limits on server space, bandwidth, number of customers, and product ranges. Ask for suitable payment milestones to ensure it meets your plans and lets you verify the progress at definite intervals. And ask about the payment terms and set out a precise payment plan with one-time and recurring fees, if any.

Negotiate to pay using your preferred payment methods such as bank wire transfer or credit card.

C. How is the software continually upgrading itself to stay ahead of market changes? Are upgrades delivered for free?

As every online business evolves and grows with time, the solution you choose must be progressive. If your web-to-print software provider is not continually upgrading the system, they are not the right fit for your online printing business.

The last thing you need is to be stuck with a vendor who does not upgrade the software as the technology evolves. Make sure new releases are coming out regularly, with great new features and bug fixes in every release.

Make sure you team up with a vendor that wants to see your online printing company grow and help you achieve unparalleled success year on year. Consult with your vendor about their upgrade policy. Ask for the process and fee involved to maintain your website with all recent software updates released by them periodically.

D. Will my team and I have access to a dedicated support team?

If the vendor you consider does not have a dedicated support team and a knowledge base comprising video tutorials, user manuals, and checklists, you should reconsider your options. If this is your first brush with web-to-print technology, you should be able to get your queries resolved promptly and efficiently. Time is money, after all.

You may need constant help during your website's setup and initial go-live phase; check the support hours - as it should match your time zone - and ask for the most efficient way to submit support requests and track its status.

Be very clear about the type of support you will receive from your vendor. You don't want to be stuck without help.

EXERCISE #9

Based on our extensive experience as a leading web-to-print software provider, we have put together a checklist that will assist you in the vendor selection process.

DATE:

VENDOR:

MY QUESTION	THEIR ANSWER	RATING [1/10]
CAN YOU PLEASE ELABORATE ON YOUR BUSINESS MODELS (ON-PREMISES OR SAAS), PRICING AND PAYMENT TERMS?		
WHAT IS YOUR IMPLEMENTATION PROCESS? AND WHAT SORT OF TRAINING WILL BE OFFERED TO MY TEAM?		
CAN YOU SHARE SOME OF YOUR SUCCESSFUL LIVE IMPLEMENTATIONS AND CUSTOMER REFERENCES WE CAN SPEAK TO?		
WHAT IS YOUR SOFTWARE UPGRADE POLICY? WHAT IS YOUR TYPICAL UPGRADE CYCLE AND ARE UPGRADES AVAILABLE FOR FREE?		
WHAT IS YOUR SUPPORT POLICY? WILL MY TEAM AND I HAVE ACCESS TO A DEDICATED SUPPORT PERSON IN OUR TIME ZONE?		
	TOTAL POINTS	
	FINAL VERDICT	YES / NO / MAYBE

PRO TIP: LET A REPRESENTATIVE FROM DESIGN'N'BUY TAKE THE CHECKLIST TEST. IF WE PASS, JOIN THE WEB-TO-PRINT BANDWAGON AND PARTNER WITH US. SIMPLE!

IDENTIFY RISKS

It is a good idea to create a risk register as early as possible in the planning phase to identify known risks and take steps to minimize them. A risk can be any high-value priority creeping in, someone on the project team leaving, seasonal breaks hampering the workflow (for e.g., Christmas), and others.

LIST THE POTENTIAL RISKS THAT CAN CROP UP DURING AND AFTER THE IMPLEMENTATION PHASE

1

2

3

4

5

TIP: CIRCULATE THIS SHEET AMONGST YOUR TEAM MEMBERS AND ALSO ASK THEM TO ADD TO IT. IT IS IMPORTANT TO CONSIDER EVERYONE'S DOUBTS AT THIS STAGE, SO THAT YOU CAN SET ADEQUATE STRATEGIES IN PLACE FOR RISK MITIGATION.

PROJECT
EXECUTION PHASE

Once you have finalized a web-to-print software provider, appoint one person in your team from the IT department as the *project owner* to liaise with them. This person will coordinate with the software vendor for any information related to the product, feedback, and approval at various stages of the implementation.

Ensuring that the web-to-print vendor also shares the kick-off document containing the details for starting the project is also the project owner's responsibility.

It is only after the Contact Person is decided and allocated responsibilities that you should start the implementation, which brings us to the next point, i.e., understanding the various aspects of the project execution phase.

13 Steps to Project Execution Phase

1 Project planning and milestones

2 Status checking and approval process

3 Server setup and configuration

4 Data collection and store population

5 Payment gateway finalization and setup

6 Shipping and delivery setup

7 Team Training and on-boarding

8 Internal and external testing

9 Important checklist before go-live

10 Marketing and SEO

11 Go Live

12 Existing client training

13 On-boarding existing clients

Once you finalize your web-to-print provider, appoint one person in your team from IT department as a "Project Owner" to liaise with them. This person will co-ordinate with software vendor for any information related to the product ,feedback and approval at the various stages of implementation.

Ensuring that the software vendor also shares the kick-off document, containing the details for starting the project, is also the responsibility of project owner. ,

" THOSE WHO PLAN DO BETTER THAN THOSE WHO DO NOT PLAN, EVEN THOUGH THEY RARELY STICK TO THEIR PLAN " - WINSTON CHURCHILL

Project Planning and Milestones

This is when the web-to-print vendor shares the entire project plan; it includes setting deadlines against each milestone and stating all dependencies from your side. You should provide all the required information on time to complete the project.

Your vendor could also use project management tools such as Zoho, Trello, or Basecamp for effective collaboration. The use of such tools centralizes communication and reduces reliance on emails and keeps it transparent, and has everyone on the same page.

Status Checking and Approval Process

The project owner should stay in touch with the web-to-print software provider team. After all, communication and collaboration are critical to the success of any project. The vendor will always check in with you and ask for your approval for each milestone they release.

The project owner will talk to all your team members and then give the required feedback or input to the vendor.

Server Setup and Configuration – Security, Backup Policy, Monitoring

For the project to be executed successfully, you need to be aware of the technical requirements of your online printing website, as that will help you in smooth server setup and configuration.

A. Server specification

This is based on the number of website visits in a day, including the number of concurrent visitors. The web page loading speed is critical for successful conversions and high Google rankings.

The server plays a significant role in bringing the page load speed below three seconds. CDN and caching mechanisms should be configured on the server to meet the desired website performance.

The vendor will suggest the required operating system, CPU and hardware configuration, RAM, and bandwidth for the server once they estimate the website visitors.

B. Server providers

These days, the cloud server or VPS server is the preferred choice of businesses where computing requirements can increase and decrease at run time. Amazon AWS and Digital Ocean are leading cloud service providers. You should choose one after carefully considering the server specification given by your software vendor. Signing up for a demo will help you.

C. Managed server service

If you do not have an in-house person to set up and manage your server infrastructure, better look for it outside. Many web-to-print vendors also provide managed server services. You can either go with your vendor or hire another agency. When deciding, make sure they offer 24/7 security, backup, and monitoring services.

> *Rather than allowing your internal team to manage it, partner with an agency that offers turnkey solutions for managed servers.*

In addition, you should set up separate development, staging, and live server environments so that you can test every release on staging before it is deployed on your live server. This will reduce any chances of errors and disruptions on your online website.

Share server details with your web-to-print vendor so that they can release the beta version of the release for User Acceptance Testing (UAT) before making the changes live.

Data Collection and Store Population

Merely implementing web-to-print technology is not enough. You need to share specific data points with the vendor to populate your website. That brings us to the six necessary elements that your team should prepare during the execution phase:

A. Graphics and images

Providing the company logo, homepage banners, and other brand specifications to the vendor is the first thing you need to kick off the project. Share the source files with them so that they can use the same font and color throughout the website implementation.

In case you don't have a logo yet, then ask the vendor for the same and check if creating one is a part of the scope of work in the contract or not. If the logo is not part of their agreement, then outsource it to the vendor or hire the services of a graphic design studio - whichever fits your budget and timeline.

Similarly, you can choose the same route to sort out the web page banners, category page designs, and other graphics you may need for the website. All the visual content should follow the brand guidelines. Make sure there is consistency in all graphics and images.

B. Identify keywords relevant to you

Make a list of the keywords that your end customers may use to search your services. You can use a range of keyword tools such as SEMRush, WordStream, KWFinder.com, and Keyword Tool. Consider the search volume and the level of competition before picking a keyword. High search volume and low competition should be your preference.

Finalize keywords for the homepage, category pages, and individual product pages. Create an excel sheet where you can list all the keywords for every page and later use it to track the ranking in the same excel sheet.

C. Content writing for website

Content is the essence of every website across industries in this day and age. Your site will look bland without the written word, and it won't fetch you the search results you desire. Here is what you should focus on during the implementation:

i. **CMS pages**

While your web-to-print software provider works on the implementation, you can start working on the website content. Keep the keywords in mind while writing the content. You can hire a freelance creative content writer to help. Alternatively, there are many portals, such as Fiverr.com and Upwork, where you can post your content requirements and ask for a quote.

ii. **Product description**

Product descriptions are the trickiest to write because they have the ultimate power to attract potential customers. To get started, list all products in an excel sheet and their keywords and write the descriptions.

iii. **Initial blog entries**

Every new website today should have a series of blog posts when launched. It helps in achieving high search rankings and in offering potential end customers something other than the products.

Find out what topics are trending in your industry, using tools such as BuzzSumo and SEMRush, and blog about them. Alternatively, write how your web-to-print software can add value to your potential customers.

D. Prepare a catalog sheet and product entries

While the web-to-print vendor continues to do their job, ask them for a product sheet format so that you can provide a list of products for them to import into the system at once. Make sure the details fed into the sheet are without any mistakes. This is a simple but tedious task as it requires manual human intervention.

E. Configure the product pricing

Convey your pricing formula to the vendor so that they can implement it in the web-to-print software. Note that you may have different pricing for different products.

For example, the price for screen printing will be defined by the number of colors in the artwork to be printed and the artwork size and number of stitches for embroidery. In contrast, your digital printing charges could be fixed on the quantity. Therefore, you need to convey your price list for all products in advance so that the vendor doesn't make any mistakes while implementing the technology.

F. Create design templates

We advise you to launch your web-to-print storefront with as many templates as possible. While the implementation phase is going on, hire a graphic designer or partner with a design team for creating professional and unique design templates that can make your printing store stand apart from your competitors. Alternatively, you can even ask the vendor if they provide the service. But before any graphics are created, you must sit down with the vendor to understand:

- the template creation process
- what design file format the software supports
- whether or not you can import your existing graphic design files, such as InDesign, PSD, or SVG, directly into the system.

You can discuss the template creation strategy with them, including whether they use design software such as Adobe Photoshop or InDesign or create designs directly in the web-to-print software using the template builder.

Have an in-depth conversation with your vendor. You can also use online image libraries such as Freepik for graphic designs, vector art, and stock photographs. Templates make submitting print orders easy for your end customers. They need to choose the artwork, edit the text and images on the website, and preview the final artwork before placing the order.

Client convenience increases sales. Therefore, keep your target audience and industry in mind, and create templates to make their lives easy.

G. Collect client testimonials and reviews for the website

If you are already in the print business, you may ask your existing end customers to give testimonials in text or video format to put on your website. You can also ask for their photographs.

Testimonials with client photos create a more substantial impact on website visitors and influence their buying decision. You can also collect reviews on third-party platforms such as Trustpilot, YELP, PowerReviews, your Facebook page, or the Google Business listing.

Payment Gateway Finalization and Setup

Constant cash flow is the lifeline of any business. That means you have to make the checkout process easy for your potential customers. They do not want to be bogged down by hidden shipping costs or, more importantly, a lack of payment options.

Choose the payment gateway that is most acceptable in your region or country. For example, in North America, Stripe and PayPal are very good. Also, talk to your bank about their options. You can also negotiate with the payment gateway providers on their fees based on your transaction volume.

Confirm with your web-to-print software provider the payment gateways they support, and check if they can integrate the system with your chosen payment gateway. Ideally, your finance department should take the initiative and sort it out.

Shipping and Delivery Setup

Once the payment gateway has been set up, choose a logistics provider. Configure their shipping costs in the system. This is so that the end customer is not kept in the dark while completing the checkout process and knows the shipping charges beforehand.

The logistics partner can also provide APIs for live shipping rates as United Parcel Service and United States Postal Service do.

Automation is essential once you start receiving a high volume of orders. Using the application program interface, the logistics partner can be aware of the orders that need to be picked up and delivered and by when.

Team Training and Onboarding

After getting approval for each milestone release, the web-to-print software provider makes the project available for UAT. But before that, they conduct training programs for you and your team so that you all can be made aware of the new changes.

The training usually takes place via Skype, Zoom, or GoToMeeting. Many vendors divide the training session into various parts so that the new information can be easily consumed. You can ask your web-to-print software provider to record these training sessions for your team so that they can refer to them at a later date if the need arises.

Your project owner needs to ensure that everyone from the team is available for the training. Their input and feedback are essential for successful implementation.

Internal and External Testing

Once the training is complete, create a real-time work environment in the system. This could include building workflows for products, departments, and teams in respective departments and creating login credentials for each person who will work on the system regularly.

EXERCISE #10

MAKE SURE THAT EACH FUNCTION OF THE PROJECT IS APPROPRIATELY CHECKED. FILL OUT THE TABLE BELOW, AND SPECIFY THE POINT OF CONTACT (POC) FROM EACH DEPARTMENT THAT IS GOING TO USE THE SYSTEM. CREATE LOGIN CREDENTIALS FOR THEM, AND THEN CONFIRM IF THE SYSTEM HAS BEEN ADEQUATELY VETTED OR NOT.

DEPARTMENT	POC	CREDENTIALS	STATUS
The digital marketing team can oversee the content organization, graphic design requirements, and branding aspects of the project.			
The accounting team can ensure that invoicing, taxation, order management, and customer accounting are in order.			
The pre-press team can check whether the artwork files they receive are acceptable or not. Example: Are they print-ready and in the preferred format? Tip: They can submit a few dummy orders and have a complete mock drill on the system.			
The production team can check the entire order life cycle with dummy order submissions. They can test the whole workflow and how the order flows within all departments. Example: Is every designated system user able to schedule and see the dashboard with the jobs which they need to process? Is role-based access working? Tip: Check the end-to-end process to avoid any surprises when you start working in live production.			
The logistics team can confirm if they can see the orders which are ready for shipment.			

Tip: Once the credentials have been created, make sure they are stored safely on the drive and this sheet is accessible to only a handful of people.

Important Checklist before Go-Live

Before launching your web-to-print storefront, make sure you keep the following things in mind:

A. Website performance

Did you know that 53 percent of mobile users leave a site that takes longer than three seconds to load? [Google] That's correct! Page speed has a direct impact on sales and conversion. The better the speed, the higher the conversion of website visitors into customers.

Because of the importance of page speed on user experience, Google rolled out a new page speed update in their algorithm in July 2018. The tech giant gives great weight to those web pages with better page speed than those slow in loading.

You should also use a benchmark of three seconds for your website. Here is a list of best practices that can be applied for better web performance:

i.   Enable browser caching. That way, the main components of a webpage can be saved in temporary storage, and the browser can easily open the webpage without having to send another HTTP request the next time the user comes back to it.

ii. Limit and remove plugins. Only keep those high-quality plugins that your online printing website needs.

iii. Minimize your CSS code. The more CSS files you have on your website, the more HTTP requests it is forced to make, thus slowing down the site.

iv. Minimize your 301 redirects. The process creates a series of links that your browser must pass through to land on the new URL, thus slowing down the webpage loading speed.

v. Optimize web images. Rescale them using tools such as TinyPNG.

B. Device and browser compatibility

Device and browser responsiveness is essential. Mobile commerce sales already accounted for 54 percent of the total e-commerce sales in 2021. If your website doesn't work well on a mobile browser or is not compatible, then you may lose half of your sales.

With the help of web-to-print technology, you can ensure your storefront is responsive on all browsers such as Chrome, Firefox, and IE and across all devices such as desktop, mobile, and tablet. The convenience of your customer base is everything.

C. Initial feedback from clients, team, and friends

Once you are ready for launch, share the website URL amongst your team members, friends, and family so that they can give their points of view. But don't just email them asking them to buy from you. Instead, provide them with a coupon code that they can use to purchase a printed item.

Once they are done shopping and receive the order from you, send them a short questionnaire. The survey can be created on SurveyMonkey or Google Forms. Compile the feedback received and check what changes can happen quickly with the project team.

You can also approach your loyal end customers in the same manner and take their feedback on what they think about the new system.

COLLECT FEEDBACKS FOR WEB2PRINT

SEND THE QUESTIONNAIRE **BELOW** TO CLIENTS, TEAM, AND FRIENDS AND COLLECT THEIR FEEDBACK

1. On a scale from 1 to 10, how would you rate our new web-to-print storefront?

1 2 3 4 5 6 7 8 9 10

2. What was the biggest hurdle you faced when navigating through the website?

3. How would you rate the checkout process?

1 2 3 4 5 6 7 8 9 10

4. How would you rate the personalization experience offered on the website?

1 2 3 4 5 6 7 8 9 10

5. Any other feedback?

Marketing and SEO

Marketing is a valuable tool for earning customer trust, generating site traffic, nurturing qualified leads, and more. Therefore, when you launch your storefront, make sure your content is SEO-optimized and geared towards the target audience.

A. Identify keywords relevant to you

Make a list of the keywords that your end customers may use to search your services. Consider the search volume and the level of competition of the keywords. You can use a range of keyword tools such as SEMRush, WordStream, KWFinder.com, and Keyword Tool.

Finalize words for the homepage, category pages, and individual product pages. Create an excel sheet where you can list all the keywords for every page and later use it to track the ranking in the same excel sheet.

Here is an example of the keywords most popularly used in the print industry:

TOP KEYWORDS USED IN PRINT INDUSTRY

KEYWORDS	SEARCH VOLUME
SUBLIMATION PRINTER	60500
VINYL PRINTER	18100
BEST PHOTO PRINTER	14800
COMMERCIAL PRINTERS	8100
DIGITAL PRINTING	9900
DIGITAL PRINTING COMPANY	170
DIGITAL PRINTING SOLUTIONS	880
ONLINE PRINTING	3600
ONLINE PRINTING SERVICES	6600
SMALL BUSINESS PRINTERS	880

B. Write meta descriptions and titles for product and category pages

Once you have finalized the keywords, the next step is to finish writing the SEO-focused copy. Writing meta descriptions and titles is an art because you have to explain a specific page in an attractive manner, but you also have to do it within a set character limit.

Put primary keywords in the page title and the secondary keywords in the description. We did it for our homepage, as shown below.

Source: Google SERP Tool

The best practice is to write to cover most of your page keywords in the title and meta description without stuffing them. The title should not be more than 60 characters, and descriptions should not be more than 156 characters.

C. Get the proper page structure

Once you have the keywords, you need to target and have written meta titles and descriptions for each page; you should focus on creating structured pages on your existing website.

Let us quickly go through H1, H2, and H3 heading formats and how they are essential for local SEO to improve your website rankings on search engines.

First things first: The headings make browsing through the website easier for consumers. When they find the title tags and heading phrases to be the same, they can relate to the content better and are more likely to pursue the website more.

Search engines present results to users based on the keywords they used to search, appropriate keyword density, and relevancy of the same on your website.

D. Set up the initial email format and design

Make sure that all of your transactional emails reflect your brand guidelines before you go live. From Order Email, Shipment Email, and Invoice Email to Customer Registration Email and Forgot Password Email - the content should also include your company details.

Also, design a few promo emails and newsletters beforehand so that you only have to customize the content later before scheduling them.

Go-Live

Once all checkpoints are met, you can ask your web-to-print software provider to launch your new website. After that is done, ask them to submit dummy orders and ensure there is no hiccup in the checkout process.

Existing Client Training

After you have done the preliminary testing, request your existing end customers to try out the website and arrange a live training session for them on how to use the new system. Also, ask them to sign up on it and create user accounts.

Onboarding Existing Clients

Change is often met with resistance, so don't be surprised if your end customers find it troublesome to use the web-to-print software. Therefore, when you share the website URL, also give them a coupon code that they can use to purchase a printed item. Whenever they place an order from their systems, give them a referral code, a coupon code, or run a Buy One Get On Free (BOGO) sale.

Incentivizing always works to get people to shop for something from you quickly. After all - who doesn't love discounts or freebies?

THE BUILD
PHASE

This is the phase where your web-to-print technology is installed and available for use by your potential customers. It is also when you start building your online customer base. Now they can initiate transactions at the new storefront. However, that is not all.

This phase is crucial for your online printing business as this is where you will get to see how well the technology is performing for you and even make tweaks along the way to ensure a smooth buying experience. There are many *go-live* strategies you can deploy, depending on what is right for your business. Your web-to-print software vendor can help you select and execute the right one.

In many cases, you can enter the go-live phase by:

- Launching with the necessary modules and then adding others in staged steps;
- Launching all modules for only one or two customers;
- Launching the entire storefront at one time for all customers - although this option is not advised.

Whichever option you choose, your online printing company must also market to boost your web-to-print storefront's visibility and get more consumers to shop with you. Use the following guidelines.

Generate Awareness through Promotions and Email

It is essential to have a schedule for any pre-launch promotional activity. While the exact timelines may differ from company to company, the best practice is to start promoting your web-to-print storefront at least a month before the launch.

Apart from email and social media teasers, promotional activities such as early-bird discounts for pre-ordering or online giveaways are effective ways to generate a buzz about your latest offering among your potential customers. Time the launch date carefully – scheduling it around periods when people shop more than usual, such as festivals and holidays, or events such as a trade show can generate the extra buzz.

Ongoing Digital Marketing

Every business today must dip its toes in the digital marketing pond. If you want to maximize the promotions of your web-to-print technology, you must leverage digital marketing in the right way. Here's how you can do so:

A. Link building

This involves linking to reliable, highly-ranked websites on your web pages and eventually getting those websites to link back to your site. An excellent way to build links is by referencing other websites and then guest posting for them in return for a backlink.

Moz.com describes link building as the practice of earning links to your web pages to boost your site's authority in search engines. There are many link building techniques that you can apply to your web-to-print store:

- List your online printing business on popular business listing websites such as Google My Business, Yelp, Foursquare, and more. You can even check out local directories such as Yellowpages and Europages. See below:

TOP BUSINESS LISTING WEBSITES

- biz.yelp.com
- showmelocal.com
- foursquare.com
- crunchbase.com
- mapquest.com
- yellowpages.com
- citysearch.com
- superpages.com
- yellowbot.com
- 192.com
- 2findlocal.com
- google.com/business/
- manta.com

- You can offer to write guest posts for high-authority websites in multiple domains such as e-commerce, print, and business. Local search engines trust mentions about businesses on local blogs, and they help generate results based on their relevance.

- Search engines also crawl local business directories to get results for local business providers. Take https://www.ohiobiz.com/ for Ohio, USA, as an example. You can find out about related sites if your business is set up in some other city or state.

- There are many governing bodies, unions, and associations for almost every industry. Get yourself listed on these sites as it helps boost credibility and exposure in front of the relevant audience.

B. Content marketing

Content marketing focuses on not just creating different content assets useful for the target audience but also marketing it on channels on which they are most active. Effective content marketing is essential to ensure that your potential customers sustain their interest in the solution.

You can create infographics, e-books, whitepapers, MS PowerPoint files, videos, case studies, and more that can be used as lead magnets on your web-to-print storefront or by submitting to high-authority syndication platforms. For example, PowerPoint decks are generally posted on Slideshare, videos are uploaded on YouTube or Vimeo, and e-books can be uploaded on your website or submitted to relevant third-party websites.

Visual content is ideal for most social media platforms and can include infographics that explain what your web-to-print technology is all about. LinkedIn, Facebook, and Twitter groups are excellent tools to promote content organically. User-generated content such as posts built around a company-specific product hashtag can also work well. Brainstorm a couple of ideas with your in-house team and decide on a hashtag that best fits your newest launch.

To boost visibility, conduct contests on social media and even ask your employees to amplify the reach of the contest.

Another avenue to explore is influencer marketing, where online bloggers create content about the product or service and share it with their online followers. This approach might take a bit of time and often works best when you partner with a marketing agency that specializes in influencer marketing so they can connect you with industry influencers on your behalf.

C. Blog posting

Maintaining a high-quality company blog is one of the best ways to consistently create and share content your potential customers will want to read and share. Blog posts should talk about the company, the product, and its uses, address commonly asked questions, or share relevant insights about how businesses can benefit from web-to-print technology.

A customer-friendly blog post is the most likely to be shared. Consider building a resource bank - launch an e-book series addressing questions and queries around printing services or the product catalog you provide.

D. Social media promotion

You shouldn't neglect social media. Registering on social media platforms such as Facebook, Twitter, LinkedIn, Instagram, Pinterest, TikTok, and YouTube lets you take your web-to-print storefront to consumers across the globe. You can place your offers, promote new products and blog posts, share new testimonials, and more on social media to engage with your customers. If your marketing budget permits, you can instantly run paid ads and reach a broader, more relevant target audience.

The importance of social media can't be stressed enough. Set up pages or accounts on every social media platform relevant to your business. Complete the profiles by submitting necessary information such as business hours, address, email address, and your web-to-print store URL.

Use a legible logo for all social media profiles, and also create a cover photo featuring your latest offer or new product range. In addition, set up Facebook Messenger on your Facebook page so that consumers can get in touch with you instantly. Create a social media calendar so that you know what to post and when. Take the time to research the best recommendations for when to post and monitor when you get the best response.

For example, some research shows that Thursday to Sunday from 1 pm to 4 pm in the target timezone works best for Facebook. Whereas Twitter is widely used from Monday to Thursday (12 to 3 pm and 5 pm). LinkedIn users are most active on Tuesday and Thursday (5 pm to 6 pm).

Include your social media buttons in every touchpoint with customers to increase follower count.

E. Press release and media coverage

Public relations is vital to the successful marketing of any new product or service. If you are leveraging a technology that will make the buying experience of your potential customer base smoother, then you must spend some time boosting your Public Relations (PR).

You can approach press representatives for website/shopping reviews or partner with media agencies to get promotional articles placed in the top online publications such as **Entrepreneur Magazine** and **Forbes**. Another option is to hold a launch event where members of the press are invited so that you can give an overview of your web-to-print storefront and address the questions of the attendees.

F. Video promotion

Many internet users enjoy watching videos no matter where they are. In fact, 85 percent of US-based internet users admit watching video content on their electronic devices. [Statista] Knowing that, use video content to attract and engage consumers. It can be much better than lengthy text content, especially when explaining a new technology. Videos are also much more shareable online.

An interesting explainer video - describing your service and why it matters - can help generate interest in your online printing company quickly. The video you produce can be shared on networks such as YouTube or Vine, and clips can be used as video ads on Facebook or Instagram. In addition, you can create a vlog (video blog) showcasing the benefits that your storefront can offer to users.

G. PPC marketing

Running paid ads on Google and major social media platforms like Facebook and Instagram can promote your service to a much larger audience. When it comes to social media, it is essential to choose platforms based on where your potential customers are most likely to be active and regularly assess each ad's performance so that resources are not wasted.

Google is the world's number one search engine. Google AdWords will fetch you good results if you go by the book. A product or service that is recommended (featured right at the top of search results) by the search engine is associated with credibility, and, of course, it also garners more clicks. Setting up a campaign on Google is easy, and you will know your way around it in no time. Google lists the necessary steps via a starter guide for beginners.

The success of your ads depends on how smartly you have picked the keywords relevant to your product or service. Therefore, research first. Use Google's paid service - Keyword Planner - to look for words and phrases your target audience might use to search for products or services similar to what you offer.

Select five to eight keywords relevant to your business. The tool will present 20 keywords similar to your search and also share an estimated cost-per-click. The more keywords you use, the more expensive your ad will be - so you might want to refrain from getting overwhelmed by the options you have.

The best part is that you only pay when a user clicks on your ad and lands on your website. Pick the most relevant keywords for your business and write strong ad copy using them. Once your ads are live, keep track of their performance daily and boost those ads that are performing well.

Order processing, monitoring, and analysis

In the initial days after the launch, it is critical to ensure that customer orders are processed quickly and accurately. Create a dedicated team to manage order fulfillment to ensure that all orders are delivered on time and that all customer queries are responded to promptly.

You should also validate that your production workflow and vendor management are working correctly and as configured. If not, make adjustments to align your application with the in-house processes.

Configure alerts and push notifications

Push notifications are clickable, rich content messages that deliver marketing or purchase-related alerts and help to boost sales. They require compelling messages that will attract your potential customers to click through to be effective.

Apart from alerts about the new launch, abandoned cart notifications, and flash sale alerts are among the most common push notifications. You can also leverage *push* technology to get customers to return to abandoned carts and complete the purchase cycle.

Logistic monitoring and analysis

A successful launch includes the timely distribution of the service to all stakeholders, sophisticated technology to track order movements, and clear accountability for each step of the process. Your supply chain team should work closely to streamline delivery processes and simplify tasks using appropriate technology.

Each role should be clearly defined, and regular checks should be conducted on the process flow to ensure that everything is moving as expected. To avoid logistics-related mishaps, try to get a few customers (maybe 10 or 20) to shop on your website and place their orders ahead of your launch. This will give you an idea about where mistakes can happen, and you can rectify them without annoying a large customer base.

Ask for customer feedback on order delivery

Customer feedback allows potential buyers to get an impartial account of how well the company delivers on its promises. Make it easy for customers to share feedback and compensate them for efforts with vouchers or discount tokens.

All feedback, positive or negative, receives a response. There are two leading platforms where feedback can be shared.

A. Social media

Social media feedback can involve customers posting about their experience and tagging the company or responding directly as a comment on the company's posts. Make sure you have someone from the customer care team address the feedback promptly.

Let the customers know using the same social media channels for every problem resolved. That shows you take complaints seriously and gives your business a good image.

B. Review platforms

These are platforms explicitly dedicated to reviewing different kinds of products and services. For instance, TripAdvisor and Yelp are review platforms for restaurants and hotels. For online printing companies, there are Google Reviews.

If your customers don't give a review on their own, reach out to them via email or phone call to ask them to provide you with feedback on Google Reviews.

The majority of businesses are slow when it comes to taking surveys. What they don't know is that 66 percent of consumers prefer giving feedback when you actively reach out to them. Be proactive. [Forbes]

You can create a survey on SurveyMonkey or Google Forms and get your customers to fill them for you. Here's what a sample survey looks like:

CUSTOMER SURVEY

1

How would you rate the quality of print?

Very High   Neither High Nor Low

High   Low   Very Low

2

Did you receive your order on time?

YES   OTHER -

NO

3

How likely are you to recommend us to a friend or colleague?

1 2 3 4 5 6 7 8 9 10

4

What other products would you like to see us offer for print?

THE GROWTH
PHASE

When Robert S. Keane launched **Vistaprint® (a CIMPRESS company)** in 1995, little did he know that it would become the world's leading provider of printing services to small businesses. Even today, Vistaprint is synonymous with low-cost personalized business cards. However, the brand is much more than that.

From selling personalized stationery, pens, and banners to labels, mugs, and photo books - the Netherlands-based company has an extensive product catalog offering. But it didn't start doing business like this. In 2011, Vistaprint pivoted and launched branded apparel, including t-shirts, jackets, sweatshirts, caps, laptop handbags, and tote bags for both men and women.

Vistaprint's journey from being a business card printer to a brand voice enabler is remarkable, and it is a fantastic example of transformation brought by web-to-print. While self-service design, proofing, and ordering are handled at the front-end through their website, the company manages controlled printing, cutting, packing, and dispatching from the back-end through its printing plants, spread across the globe, in end-to-end productions.

Today, Vistaprint is regarded as the source for high-quality graphic design, internet printing, and premium service - used by businesses and individuals. That brings us to a crucial point in this book, i.e., growth.

Even though your web-to-print technology is available for your potential customers, with operations running smoothly, it doesn't mean you should stop finding ways to pivot, disrupt, or scale your printing business.

This section will discuss eight ways any online printer can find rapid growth.

Move Beyond Printing Services

It is convenient if your web-to-print storefront enables consumers to customize and place orders on a range of products, such as stationery, t-shirts, and mugs. It is essential to be viewed as a one-stop shop, just like Vistaprint. However, you can take it further and include value-added services to the mix. These services include graphic design assistance, artwork correction, and address book preparation.

For example, if your potential customer is neither adept at personalizing artwork nor likes using any of the pre-designed templates offered and just bounces off your website, that is lost revenue. Consumers, in general, don't have time to look for options. They want help instantly.

The good news is that by giving them the option to use your graphic design services upfront, you will make their buying experience smooth and win their loyalty for life. The same goes for potential customers looking to get their artwork corrected or address books prepared.

US-based Ascend Sportswear is one of the leading providers of customized cycling jerseys and gear. If their potential customers don't have a logo and want one, then Ascend Sportswear's designers provide this service. Along with customized cycling jerseys, the company offers design support. Their web-to-print technology includes a 3D design studio for the job.

In short, offering value-added services enables you to generate extra revenue and become a provider of a 360-degree solution for your customers.

Provide Branded Private Portals

In a bid to target its B2B clientele, Vistaprint started a Brand Matching facility that enabled small businesses to seamlessly create all kinds of printed marketing products - including pens, mugs, notepads, and brochures - using the same brand colors and fonts. Creating consistent small business branding can be difficult without the right tools.

Your online printing business can grow further by offering branded private portals to your corporate clientele with preloaded design templates for items such as business cards, letterhead, and envelopes. Enable businesses to lock their brand elements to ensure brand consistency with every order.

A completely secure, private, and branded B2B corporate storefront with role-based access serves all organizational customer needs.

Find Your Niche

There are so many things that can be customized and printed – photo books, mugs, photo cards, calendars, wall art, stationery, uniforms, shoes, and others. Additionally, you may deal with multiple paper types and sizes – broadening your offerings.

Simplify what you offer and make it easy to understand. For example, if you want to focus on niche product segments and customer groups, create niche stores with a centralized back-end administration. To take the example further, you can set up a web-to-print storefront that sells photo books and photo products and a different one dedicated to selling t-shirts only.

Digitaaldrukwerk.be is an online printing company where you can order high-quality digital work. They have set up niche storefronts like Babygrafix.be for offering customized baby cards and other birth-related print online with coordinated text and images, and Communiekaarten. com, where customers can make stickers and wraps for Mentos, Sportlife, or Pringles online, along with the option to design buttons with a bottle opener or mirror. All these websites operate under a centralized application for easy administration.

Globalize to Expand Customer Reach

Often defined as the process of triggering a consumer to spend more money to buy an upgraded version of their current choice, upselling is a sales concept that could make your web-to-print storefront a success. Consumers assume that any printing company they shop with will deliver high-quality print and excellent customer service. However, there is another factor that could win you a considerable chunk of the target audience, i.e., localization.

The minute you enable your potential customers to use pre-designed templates or see a 3D preview of their designs or web content in their *preferred language*, you instantly transform their shopping experience and become a preferred commodity supplier.

To localize your products and services in each region, create different stores for each country. For example, for targeting Middle Eastern countries such as Saudi Arabia, UAE, and Kuwait, create three different versions of the website in the languages spoken in these countries, and offer local currency, payment, and shipping options.

Transform into a Print Marketplace

Transform your business gradually from being an online retail store to a marketplace. Allow graphics designers from across the globe to register and publish their designs. Define commissions for these designers and award them when print with their designs is ordered.

That way, you crowdsource designs without significant investments in an in-house design team and offer a plethora of design options (both vector art and photos) to your customers.

Remember: its unique design templates and artwork are vital to attracting and engaging customers for any printing portal. You can add any number of vendors to your online print storefront and expand your product offerings. E-commerce giant Amazon follows a similar model, which is why we always have multiple options for the same product.

Take it up a notch and integrate third-party inventory suppliers, fulfillment partners, or drop-shippers with your web-to-print storefront, and automate your ordering and dispatch workflow so that - besides giving more choices to the consumers - you also deliver promptly.

Grow Your Reseller Channels

Set up white-labeled website portals for each of your resellers so that they have the freedom to market their unique product catalog and design templates based on their target potential customers. When they can independently sell their services and get orders from you, you can reward them on a commission-to-commission basis.

Such an arrangement creates a win-win proposition for all entities as trade printers can attract more resellers, and resellers get their website for marketing their services even if they can't process the order in-house.

Execute a Properly-Planned Digital Marketing Strategy

Gone are those days when a business could be marketed on a whim. Today, having a strategy is essential to assess the effectiveness of initiatives and audience engagement, as marketing has become an expensive function. Did you know that 65 percent of the most successful content marketers have a documented strategy? Your printing company should develop one so that you know what your quarterly or bi-annual priorities are, what tools you need to do your job, and how much revenue your business should ideally generate.

While organic marketing is viewed as necessary to boost sales and grow, it is also vital to invest in paid ads. In the Project Planning and Build Phases, you should have already set up active social media accounts for your printing business.

However, in the Growth Phase, you should up the game by running paid ads on Google and Facebook. It is improbable for a consumer to buy anything on their first visit to your website. Therefore, it is important to keep showing ads in various places online. Google and Bing ads can help you achieve that visibility.

On the other hand, Facebook is the most widely used social media channel, which is bound to get you excellent traction. Do keyword research and identify the kinds of ads your competitors are running. It is best not to put all your eggs in one basket but mix and match instead.

> *Thirty percent of all internet users implemented ad blockers by the end of 2018 and early 2019. [CMI]*
>
> *The statistic is alarming, given how fast PPC adverts are mushrooming the internet space. Does that mean your printing company should not use this marketing tactic?*
>
> *No, but they should create an ad strategy first and focus on writing a good, converting copy that addresses the pain points of the potential customers and nurtures them to become converting clients of your online printing business.*

Besides running ads, you should explore referral partnerships, email marketing, and influencer engagement programs that help drive organic traffic to your website and make way for a two-way conversation with your customers.

A strategy also helps narrow the team's day-to-day tasks to increase efficiency. Your marketing team will steer their energies to those activities that support business growth and add value to your online brand.

Work with Your Web-To-Print Vendor

Like any other e-commerce business, you should build a strong network of trade printers, resellers, and designers. You should keep your customers happy and market yourself by using different methods and channels.

More importantly, for the growth of your online print store, you should coordinate with your vendor to implement the changes on your website, so they follow your growth plans. The solution you choose must be progressive.

If your web-to-print software provider is not continually upgrading the system, they are not the right fit for your online printing business. You don't want to be stuck with someone who does not update the software or doesn't upgrade or support your growth requirements.

Make sure you team up with a vendor who wants to see your online printing company grow and achieve unparalleled success.

Find your niche. Of course, many online print storefronts offer the same services. Define what makes your business stand out. Work on your weaknesses and turn them into your strengths.

Listen to your customer feedback and act upon that. Support them. Figure out where your customers face trouble on your storefront and resolve those glitches. All these actions will make your customers love you even more.

SUCCESS!

Success has no definition, so keep re-evaluating your ROI from your web-to-print investment.

Business is unpredictable. Markets are dynamic. Consumers are spoiled for choice. Due to the continuous changes, you should always measure your business performance so that you know what works and what doesn't.

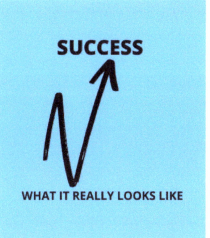

But how do you measure business success? You can call your online printing company a success even if it sells just 100 print orders in a month or you get 40 percent of your revenues through online stores, and if it integrates well with your long-term business strategy.

Merriam-Webster's dictionary defines success as the fact of getting or achieving wealth, respect or fame.

Success is a construct - an idea comprising various conceptual elements, which are typically considered subjective and not based on empirical evidence. In other words, success is not a single thing but a combination of different elements such as hard work, passion, learning from failures, and taking consistent action.

If you don't mind rolling up your sleeves and getting your hands dirty for your business, you are better off than you think. If numbers guide your appraisal of success, here are seven parameters that can help you to do so:

Client happiness index

This metric quantifies the degree to which a consumer is satisfied with a product, service, or shopping experience. It shows how your customers feel about engaging with your company. Interview your customers or take a survey for their feedback on their buying experience with you. Some of the questions could include:

CLIENT'S HAPPINESS INDEX

1

Which of the following words would you use to describe our products?

RELIABLE   OVERPRICED

HIGH QUALITY   IMPRACTICAL

USEFUL   INEFFECTIVE

UNIQUE   POOR QUALITY

VALUE FOR MONEY   UNRELIABLE

2

How likely are you to purchase any of our products again?

EXTREMELY LIKELY   NOT SO LIKELY

VERY LIKELY   NOT AT ALL LIKELY

SOMEWHAT LIKELY

Depending on the answers you receive from the survey, apply this simple formula to calculate the metric: Happy Customers/Number of Customers Asked = Happiness Index.

Number of print orders

Keep track of your print orders to see how the number has grown or decreased in a specified timeframe. You can make comparisons on a daily, weekly, monthly, quarterly, and annual basis - whatever you deem fit.

Create a spreadsheet in the cloud and give access to the relevant teams so that they can keep updating numbers regularly. If you run a Print MIS, it may be able to provide the numbers and automatically update for you.

Print production efficiency

The same logic applies to measuring your production efficiency. Keep track of your print jobs to see the impact on overall efficiency and cost reduction from back-office automation and print workflow implementation. Here also, you can make comparisons on a daily, weekly, monthly, quarterly, and annual basis.

Create a spreadsheet in the cloud and give access to the relevant teams so that they can keep updating numbers regularly. If you run a Print MIS, it may be able to provide the numbers and automatically update for you.

Overhead costs

No business is free from expenditures, and if you are spending more than you can afford, that is a cause for alarm.

Web-to-print technology minimizes the cost of manual labor, including taking orders on the phone and other time-consuming tasks such as creating artwork and proofreading. It does so by digitizing the entire buying process. Use the numbers to determine how much the overhead has gone down.

Errors and re-printing jobs

If you have reliable data about the number of print errors and re-prints before and after deploying web-to-print technology, it provides a clear picture of whether or not the technology has helped you reduce print waste.

Number of new customers

One of the most common growth metrics is the number of new customers you acquire within a specified timeframe. You can do this calculation on a monthly, quarterly, or annual basis and compare it with the numbers before you had before you deployed web-to-print technology.

Internal team feedback

Successful businesses are built with team members open to feedback and who can express opinions while working together to develop ideas and solutions for the project. Survey your internal teams from all divisions - such as sales, pre-press, post-press, shipment, and delivery - to determine whether or not web-to-print has changed their way of working for the better.

CONCLUSION

You don't have to pop open a bottle of champagne every time your actual figures surpass the estimates. But doing something as simple as having a pizza party in the office can boost everyone's morale in your team. Communicate every win - big or small - to them.

Success is built on structure and having a long-term plan to get your printing business where you want it to be. If you have a growth framework, you are already pretty successful. Most business owners don't plan!

The adage, "Action is the foundational key to all success," seems appropriate in such a scenario.

We hope you take on board some of the strategies discussed in this book and make your web-to-print storefront a smash hit. It is essential to have fun along the way! And finally, learn to enjoy the ride.

Remember: "There are no secrets to success. It is the result of preparation, hard work, and learning from failure." - Colin Powell

REFERENCES

https://www.emarketer.com/content/amazon-only-shoppers-on-the-rise?ecid=NL1014

https://www.statista.com/statistics/261676/digital-buyer-penetration-worldwide/

http://whattheythink.com/news/66257-napl-white-paper-finds-significant-gap-between-web-print-expectations-results/

https://www.paypal.com/uk/webapps/mpp/stories/media-resources

https://www.marketsandmarkets.com/Market-Reports/large-format-inkjet-printers-lfp-market-523.html

https://www.asicentral.com/news/web-exclusive/november-2018/state-of-the-decorated-apparel-industry-2018/

https://www.grandviewresearch.com/industry-analysis/decorated-apparel-market

https://www.marketwatch.com/press-release/personalized-gifts-market-expected-to-succeed-cagr-of-952-until-2023-current-business-standing-in-general-retail-goods-and-services-sector-2019-10-22

https://www.smitherspira.com/news/2016/november/growth-for-digital-textile-print-market

https://www.inkworldmagazine.com/issues/2017-07-01/view_features/the-digital-textile-market

https://www.credenceresearch.com/report/t-shirt-printing-machines-market

https://dotcomdist.com/2016-e-commerce-Packaging-Study/

https://www.smithers.com/resources/2018/may/e-commerce-a-$20-billion-market-for-corrugated

https://www.futuresource-consulting.com/reports/posts/2018/july/futuresource-consumer-photobook-market-report-western-europe-11-jul-18/?locale=en

https://www.marketresearch.com/Stratistics-Market-Research-Consulting-v4058/Tumblers-Global-Outlook-12533724/

https://www.mordorintelligence.com/industry-reports/global-print-label-market-industry

https://hbr.org/2012/04/the-new-science-of-building-great-teams

https://www.atlassian.com/teamwork

https://www.designnbuy.com/

https://www.barilliance.com/increase-average-order-value-aov/

https://www.columnfivemedia.com/work-items/infographic-no-cart-left-behind-why-shoppers-arent-following-through-on-online-purchases

http://www.countingcharacters.com/google-serp-tool

https://www.ohiobiz.com/

https://www.statista.com/statistics/272835/share-of-internet-users-who-watch-online-videos/

https://ads.google.com/home/#tab0=0

https://www.forbes.com/sites/lydiadishman/2014/03/07/retailers-your-surveys-are-making-customers-suffer/#752284a42b4f

https://contentmarketinginstitute.com/wp-content/uploads/2018/10/2019_B2B_Research_Final.pdf

AUTHOR'S BIO

NIDHI AGRAWAL

CEO & Co-founder
DESIGNNBUY, INC.

Nidhi is a visionary with profound business acumen and a management capability backed by strong technological background. Her comprehensive problem-solving skills have led to many successful online print businesses. Known for her hands-on approach, Nidhi's leadership style and her journey so far has been commended at many renowned platforms.

She has worked with print service providers from all verticals and in this book, Nidhi has shared some of key aspects of building a successful print eCommerce business.

ABHISHEK AGARWAL

Chief Business Development Officer
& Co-founder
DESIGNNBUY, INC.

Abhishek is father of a beautiful daughter and found his business partner in his life partner. He is an entrepreneur with immense experience in building successful technology businesses. A thought leader, who constantly looks for WHAT's NEXT. He builds & mentors teams to work at their best and add something new to one's mind, body, and soul daily.

This book is a culmination of his experience working with printers for more than a decade for enabling their business online that are traditionally run offline.

Notes

Notes

Notes

www.ingramcontent.com/pod-product-compliance
Lightning Source LLC
LaVergne TN
LVHW011802070326
832902LV00025B/4608